# Praise for

"Kyle Idleman is never [...] opposite. Kyle always stirs, excites, and challenges. By the end of this book you will see grace in a new light; you will see your loving God in a new light. Read it and be encouraged."

**Max Lucado**, author of *GRACE* and *In the Grip of Grace*

"Grace is my favorite topic, and Kyle Idleman's new book breathes fresh life into it through engaging stories and winsome insights. Nothing is greater than grace. Celebrate it, live it, share it!"

**Lee Strobel**, award-winning author of *The Case for Grace*

"Kyle Idleman is a remarkable writer. As he opens his heart and God's Word, he shares stories that are both moving and meaningful and confesses his own weaknesses with stunning transparency. He also has a wry sense of humor, which enhances and never detracts from the important lessons he offers. *Grace Is Greater* is practical and inspirational, providing a clear path to freedom through God's amazing gift of grace. I loved it!"

**Liz Curtis Higgs**, bestselling author of *Bad Girls of the Bible*

"As a follower of Jesus, I can't help but being a fan of Kyle Idleman. He seems to eat, sleep, and breathe a passion for heart-connection with God. That kind of a relationship can't happen when we confine God's grace to the work he did to save us. It happens when we allow his grace to permeate the messiest parts of our lives and ultimately become the defining feature of how we treat others. Kyle's book *Grace Is Greater* is a journey in how to make that happen."

**Dr. Tim Kimmel**, author of *Grace Based Parenting* and *Grace Filled Marriage*

"If Kyle Idleman writes something, I read it! I sat down to read *Grace Is Greater* and couldn't put it down. His teaching on grace challenged me. The way God is presented comforted me. The words that describe people inspired me! I'm different and better because of this book . . . and you will be too."

**Caleb Kaltenbach**, author of *Messy Grace*

"When I was sent the manuscript for *Grace Is Greater*, I thought, *Oh no, not another book on grace!* I quickly checked my little library and discovered that I already had at least eight books whose titles included the word *grace*. I asked myself, *Do I need another one?* But I began to read and was immediately drawn in by Kyle Idleman's engaging stories, delightful humor, compelling truths, and, yes, grace. I laughed out loud and shed a few tears as I was reminded in fresh ways of the all-encompassing greatness, power, and relevance of God's grace for the brokenness, disappointments, and hurts we all encounter on our journey. After reading *Grace Is Greater*, I decided the answer to my question was, *Yes, I do need another book on grace.* I think we all do."

**Cynthia Heald**, author of *Becoming a Woman of Grace*

# THE
# GRACE
## EFFECT

What Happens When Our Brokenness
Collides with God's Grace

# kyle idleman

## BakerBooks

a division of Baker Publishing Group
Grand Rapids, Michigan

© 2017 by Kyle Idleman

Published by Baker Books
a division of Baker Publishing Group
P.O. Box 6287, Grand Rapids, MI 49516-6287
www.bakerbooks.com

Printed in the United States of America

Library of Congress Cataloging-in-Publication Data is on file at the Library of Congress, Washington, DC.

978-0-8010-7298-7

Unless otherwise indicated, Scripture quotations are from the Holy Bible, New International Version®. NIV®. Copyright © 1973, 1978, 1984, 2011 by Biblica, Inc.™ Used by permission of Zondervan. All rights reserved worldwide. www.zondervan.com

Scripture quotations labeled Message are from THE MESSAGE. Copyright © by Eugene H. Peterson 1993, 1994, 1995, 1996, 2000, 2001, 2002. Used by permission of NavPress. All rights reserved. Represented by Tyndale House Publishers, Inc.

Scripture quotations labeled NLT are from the *Holy Bible*, New Living Translation, copyright © 1996, 2004, 2015 by Tyndale House Foundation. Used by permission of Tyndale House Publishers, Inc., Carol Stream, Illinois 60188. All rights reserved.

Published in association with Don Gates of the literary agency The Gates Group, www.the-gates-group.com.

Some of the names and details of people referenced in this book have been changed to protect the privacy of those involved.

17  18  19  20  21  22  23      7  6  5  4  3  2  1

# Contents

# 1

# More Forgiving
# Than Your Guilt

My son has always taken Halloween trick-or-treating very seriously.* He literally maps out the neighborhood, carefully routing his course so he doesn't miss a single house. This is not about having fun collecting candy. This is a competition to be won, a mission to complete. He chooses his costumes for mobility purposes. At the end of each competition, he brings his bag of candy in and weighs it. Then he organizes it. He gets that impulse from his momma. He separates all the chocolates and freezes them. He organizes the rest by kind and color.

*If you're already upset because I let my son trick-or-treat, please remember that you're reading about grace.

I knew all that. What I *didn't* know is that he also creates a spreadsheet to track how many pieces of candy he has collected, how many he has eaten, and how many he has left.

When he was nine years old, his bag weighed in at 5.8 pounds. He went to bed that Halloween night and I did what I normally do—stole a young child's treasure while he slept. I decided he'd never notice if a few pieces of Laffy Taffy went missing, so I took three pieces and destroyed the evidence. The next day I came home from work, opened the front door, and found he was waiting for me. He said, "Dad, we need to talk." He sat me down and asked, "Is there anything you'd like to tell me?" I was now feeling a little nervous and wondered if my wife sold me out.* Then he pulled out a piece of paper with numbers and symbols I couldn't decode, looked me in the eye, and told me he knew I'd eaten three pieces of taffy.

I never thought I'd get caught, but it turns out he was keeping track of his candy. I would have denied it to my son, but his evidence was strong and this was not my first offense. Instead of telling him I was sorry, I took the opportunity to point out some details to my son that he may have overlooked. For example, that I made his existence possible.

*He probably paid her off with Junior Mints.

Obviously a few pieces of candy aren't that big of a deal, but here's what I discovered about myself in that moment: when I'm guilty of something, even if it's not a big deal, I have a tendency to be defensive. I do not like to admit guilt. I will passionately defend myself, irrationally justify myself, and almost always minimize the seriousness of what I've done.

If that's how I respond to being accused of stealing three pieces of Laffy Taffy, chances are I'm not going to respond with much honesty or humility when it comes to the sin in my life. Everything in me wants to deny, compare, minimize, and justify. But as long as I approach my sin with that kind of spirit, I won't be able to experience the power and greatness of God's grace.

## The Ugly Truth

Our ability to appreciate grace is in direct correlation to the degree to which we acknowledge our need for it. The more I recognize the ugliness of my sin, the more I can appreciate the beauty of God's grace. The Bible holds up a mirror and confronts us with the reality of our sin.

> Everyone has sinned; we all fall short of God's glorious standard. (Rom. 3:23 NLT)

So who does "everyone" include? Well, everyone includes you and everyone includes me. We have all sinned.

I'm sure you've heard that before. I doubt it's new information. My question is, how do you respond to that information? For a long time I would read verses like that and think to myself, *Well, yeah. I mean, technically, I've sinned. But I haven't sin* sinned.

Here's the way it usually gets worded to me: "I'm not *that* bad."

My wife and I were eating dinner together at a restaurant when a woman, probably in her late fifties, came over and introduced herself. She began to tell her story of how she had recently become a Christian. Except she didn't say "Christian," she said "follower of Jesus." She pointed out her husband seated at a table across the restaurant. I think she felt like she needed to address why he didn't come with her to say hello. She explained he wasn't upset about her decision but seemed annoyed by it and didn't understand. I smiled and waved at him. He waved but didn't smile. His wave was like the wave you give the other driver at a four-way stop when you tell them to go ahead even though you think you have the right-of-way. That kind of wave. I

> *The more I recognize the ugliness of my sin, the more I can appreciate the beauty of God's grace.*

went over and introduced myself, and we chatted for a minute or two.

The next day I followed up with an email to both of them saying it was good to meet them and to let me know if either of them had any questions I could help with. I didn't hear anything back for a couple of months. And then one day I was sitting at my desk when I got an email from the husband. He told me about the changes he had seen in his wife. She was kinder and more patient. She seemed more joyful. But instead of being excited about these changes, he was skeptical. Here's a line from his email: "She seems much happier now, but I think she's just trying to get me to drink the Kool-Aid."

I knew that this wasn't a rhetorical email. He was reaching out but didn't want to say it. I emailed him back and asked if he would come to church with his wife and visit with me for a few minutes after a service.

We sat in a small room, and I began to tell him the Good News of the gospel. I began with Romans 3:23 and made the point that everyone has sinned and fallen short of God's standard. Immediately he became defensive and said, "I'm not that bad. Most people would consider me a good man." He thought it unfair to be called a sinner and be judged by "God's standard."

"How fair is it to set a standard that no one can meet and then say everyone is a sinner?" he continued. "It's like setting up a target that's out of range and then blaming the shooter for not being able to hit it."

I started my attempt at a theological explanation of why we were sinners. I was going to begin with Adam and Eve in the Garden of Eden and talk about how sin entered the world. I think he would have been impressed with some of the terms I was going to use to explain how we have rebelled against God. But before I had a chance to talk about imputation or ancestral sin, his wife interrupted me and asked if she could say something.

*As long as we think I'm not that bad, grace will never seem that good.*

She didn't wait for my permission. She turned toward her husband and said, "Do you think it's OK to get drunk and yell at your spouse? Do you think it's OK to lie about your sales numbers? Do you think it's OK to tell your grandson you'll be at his game and then not show up?" And she asked three or four more personal questions that were clearly indicting. His answers to these questions were obvious. Then she said, "You say it's not fair to be held to God's standard, but you fall short of your own standards."

I had never thought of it that way. We may get defensive when a preacher calls us a sinner—but forget about God's standard; we can't even meet our own standards.

We work hard at convincing ourselves and others we're not that bad, but the truth is we are worse than we ever imagined. The more you push back on that, the more you push back on experiencing God's grace. If we miss the reality and the depth of our sin, we miss out on the grace of God.

As long as we think *I'm not that bad*, grace will never seem that good. We usually come to the conclusion that we are not that bad a couple of different ways.

### 1. We compare ourselves to others.

It's not that we claim to be perfect, but when we compare ourselves with others, what we have done doesn't seem to be that big of a deal. And of course, when we are judging ourselves we usually give ourselves a big break. Compared to what a lot of people are doing, our sins amount to little more than jaywalking or loitering.

We dismiss our sin and our need for grace by comparing ourselves to others, but do you know what you're doing when you compare yourself to other people and feel superior to them? Yep, you're sinning. And it's likely that from where God sits, your pride and self-righteousness are uglier than the sins of the person you just compared yourself to.

### 2. We weigh the bad against the good.

Last year I read a *New York Times* interview with New York City's former mayor Michael Bloomberg.

At the time Bloomberg was seventy-two years old. He was being interviewed just before his fiftieth college reunion. Bloomberg talked about how sobering it was to realize how many of his classmates had passed away. But the journalist, Jeremy Peters, observed that Bloomberg didn't seem too worried about what waited for him on the other side. Peters wrote:

> But if [Bloomberg] senses that he may not have as much time left as he would like, he has little doubt about what would await him at a Judgment Day. Pointing to his work on gun safety, obesity and smoking cessation, he said with a grin: "I am telling you if there is a God, when I get to heaven I'm not stopping to be interviewed. I am heading straight in. I have earned my place in heaven. It's not even close."[1]

From his perspective grace isn't needed or wanted. He puts the good he has done on one side of the scale and decides he's not going to need any help.

We can all find ways to reach the conclusion that *I'm not that bad*, but in doing so we miss out on God's great gift of grace. Until we recognize our need for grace, we won't care about receiving it.

Our default is to cover up our sin or at the very least minimize it. But in covering up our sin we are covering up grace. In minimizing sin we are diminishing the joy that comes with forgiveness. Jesus didn't try to make people

feel better about themselves by diminishing the seriousness of their sin and falsely reassuring them that they were
not that bad. Jesus explained that the one who is forgiven
much loves much (see Luke 7:47). He paralleled our love
for God with the degree of forgiveness we have received.

## The Biggest Sinner I Know

I read a quote on Twitter the other day from a pastor
named Jean Larroux. I inwardly protested as soon as I
read it, but ironically my protest likely only did more to
prove the truth of what he said. Here's the quote: "If the
biggest sinner you know isn't you, then you don't know
yourself very well."

My immediate and instinctual response to that quote
was, *Well, look, I'm a sinner. In fact, I'm a big sinner. But
I'm not the biggest sinner I know.* But the more I think
about that quote, and the more I'm honest with myself
and my motives, the more difficulty I have denying it.

There was something about that quote that seemed
familiar to me. I couldn't quite put my finger on it until
I was rereading the familiar passage of Scripture where
Paul identifies himself to Timothy as the chief of sinners:

> Here is a trustworthy saying that deserves full accep-
> tance: Christ Jesus came into the world to save sin-
> ners—of whom I am the worst. (1 Tim. 1:15)

I remembered writing a paper about this passage when I was in seminary. My paper focused on Paul's past before he became a Christian. I made the case that Paul describes himself as the worst of sinners because he had been a persecutor of Christians and did everything he could to destroy the church and the cause of Christ. When my professor returned the paper to me, there was no grade at the top of the page. Instead, in red ink, he had written "Rewrite."

I wasn't sure what the problem was. He hadn't made any notes in the margin to help me understand why I needed to start over on the entire paper. After class I went up to his desk, hoping to get a little feedback. Then he took out his red pen and he circled one word from 1 Timothy 1:15.

> Here is a trustworthy saying that deserves full acceptance: Christ Jesus came into the world to save sinners—of whom I **am** the worst.

I waited for a moment, expecting him to expound, but he had already moved on to the next student. I stood there staring at that one word *am*. Suddenly I realized what I had missed. The verb *am* is present tense. And that changed everything. Paul didn't say, "I *was* the worst of sinners." He said, "I *am* the worst of sinners."

If you were to hook me up to a lie detector test and ask me, "Do you think you're the worst sinner?" I would probably say yes because I'm so sinful that I'll try to make myself seem more spiritual by sounding as humble as possible.* But I'm fairly certain the polygraph machine would reveal the truth. If I'm honest, deep down, probably not even that deep, I don't consider myself the worst of sinners. But I can tell you, the more I learn about the righteousness of God and the more I examine my own life and motives—the closer I'm getting to the inescapable conclusion that I am the worst sinner I know.

## The Sickness of Sin

Romans 3:23 says that everyone has sinned. Romans 6:23 says the penalty for our sin is death. We can minimize what we have done, but the Bible says we have been declared guilty and sentenced to death.

As I am writing this chapter, I have been quarantined to the guest room. I have supposedly been sick for the last few days, and I'm supposed to be resting and getting better. On the nightstand next to me is some medicine my wife brought in to me a few hours ago. But she knows I won't take it. See, despite evidence to the contrary, I'm not convinced I'm actually sick. My wife would tell you I have a problem admitting when I'm not feeling well. For as long as possible I will refuse to

*Don't judge; you're the one going around hooking people up to lie detector tests.

concede that I'm sick. . . . Hold on a sec, she's coming in to check on me.

OK, I'm back.

Here's what just happened. She came in and told me to take the medicine she had brought earlier. I asked her, "Why would I take medicine if I'm not sick?" She walked over and put her hand on my forehead and said, "You feel a little warm to me. I think you have a fever." I felt my own forehead and assured her I was fine. She suggested I let her take my temperature. So I cracked a joke about how it wouldn't be accurate, because when she walks in the room my temperature goes up several degrees. She rolled her eyes, and as she left the room she said, "Well, just remember I'm not going to be kissing you until you get better."

I took the medicine.

I refuse to acknowledge I'm sick, because if I'm sick it means I have to do some things differently. If I admit to myself I'm sick, I have to take medicine and lie in bed, and I don't like taking medicine and staying in bed. And so my strategy is to deny the reality of my condition as long as possible. But it turns out pretending I'm not sick is not a very effective way to get better. The sooner I admit my illness, the sooner I will take medicine and start feeling better. The sooner I start feeling better, the sooner I will be kissing my wife. But the longer I refuse to acknowledge my sickness and the longer I refuse to take the medicine, the longer I put off feeling better.

Around 1,600 years ago, Augustine wrote in his *Confessions*, "My sin was all the more incurable because I did not think myself a sinner."[2] Until we come face-to-face with our terminal diagnosis, we will refuse the cure.

The Bible gives us our diagnosis—we all have a sickness called *sin*. It's a virus that has infected the whole world. Romans 5:12 explains it this way:

> When Adam sinned, sin entered the world. Adam's sin brought death, so death spread to everyone, for everyone sinned. (NLT)

We've all been diagnosed with sin and our condition is terminal—*the wages of sin is death*. But then Paul introduces us to an antidote called *grace*.

> For the sin of this one man, Adam, brought death to many. But even greater is God's wonderful grace and his gift of forgiveness to many through this other man, Jesus Christ. And the result of God's gracious gift is very different from the result of that one man's sin. For Adam's sin led to condemnation, but God's free gift leads to our being made right with God. . . . For the sin of this one man, Adam, caused death to rule over many. But even greater is God's wonderful grace and his gift of righteousness, for all who receive it will live in triumph over sin and death through this one man, Jesus Christ.

Yes, Adam's one sin brings condemnation for everyone, but Christ's one act of righteousness brings a right relationship with God and new life for everyone. (vv. 15–18 NLT)

Paul sets up an equation. On one side of the equation is your sin, and your sin is worse than you can imagine. You can minimize it, rationalize it, and try to dismiss it, but you are terminally ill. On the other side of the equation is God's grace. When Jesus died on the cross his blood wasn't infected by sin, and he became the antidote that cures us. After putting your sin on one side and God's grace on the other, Paul solves the equation.

*Grace is always greater— no matter what.*

Even greater is God's wonderful grace. (v. 15 NLT)

I can tell you confidently that you've done nothing so horrible that grace can't cover it. Grace is always greater—no matter what.

## Making It Personal

One weekend in church I gave everyone a piece of paper with this equation:

$$\text{Grace} > \underline{\hspace{3cm}}$$

And I asked them to fill in the blank with their worst sin.

I'd like to ask you to take a turn at this. The only way for grace to be experienced is for you to personalize your need for it. Take a minute and fill in the blank of the equation below, and after you fill in the blank go ahead and solve the equation by circling either the "greater than" or "less than" sign.

$$\text{Grace} >/< \underline{\hspace{3cm}}$$

Paul's explanation in Romans 5 about the greatness of God's grace is really helpful. But an explanation of grace without experiencing grace is like being terminally ill and a doctor gives you lifesaving medicine but you refuse to take it.

The greatness of God's grace means I don't have to keep trying to convince myself I am "not that bad."

The truth is I am worse than I ever wanted to admit, but God's grace is greater than I ever could have imagined.

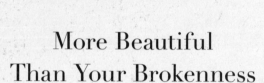

# More Beautiful
# Than Your Brokenness

In 2009 I received the following message on Facebook from a man named Wes who was in his early forties:

> I don't know if you have any good "Facebook stories" but I think you might after you read this. I'm not exactly sure why, but I feel compelled by God to tell you this story. It goes all over the place . . . so bear with me.

> I have known I was adopted all my life. I was raised in a Christian home by two terrific people who could not have children of their own. I'm now happily married and have my own children whom I dearly love.

I never had a desire to seek out my birth parents until a few years ago. I was attending a Christian retreat and one of the speakers was an older man who told about getting his girlfriend pregnant and then secretly giving the child up for adoption. He explained that he had lived with constant guilt that eventually caused him to develop a hard heart and bitterness toward God. One day his daughter contacted him and told him that she forgave him and God did too. It changed this man's life and he spoke of the freedom and the healing he had found.

That story made me think of my own situation. I wondered if it would help my birth parents to know that I was doing OK. I was able to find the name of my birth father and contacted him. It became clear to me that I was right about the guilt and pain that could follow a person after making such a difficult decision. He had never told anyone about my birth. It seemed that it was probably best that I not interfere with his life or complicate things for him.

But then something happened. . . . One night I was lying in bed with my wife and one of your shows came on. I was already half asleep, but my wife was watching it. Suddenly, I was startled when my wife exclaimed, "Oh, my God! That's your cousin!" She was talking about you. She knew a lot more about my birth family than I did because she is the one who did all the research. I didn't believe her but after a little Google search I realized she was correct.

I hope you are not too shocked, but your uncle, David Idleman, is my birth father. I picked you to contact first because

as [you are] a pastor I thought you might be used to giving
counsel on difficult situations. I know that I also have a sister,
but I don't know if she knows about me. I don't want to stir
the family pot and create problems or difficult situations,
but like I said, I felt like God compelled me to reach out.

When I read that Facebook message, immediately a
lot of things made sense to me. I had grown up close to
my uncle Dave. He taught me how to slalom water-ski
when I was a kid and gave me a few karate lessons when I
was in middle school. But as I grew older, I could tell my
uncle carried a heavy weight wherever he went. Keeping
a secret like that for so many years wearies a man. His
eyes often seemed tired to me, worn out, like he was
always just getting off a long day at work.

My uncle Dave somehow missed grace when his girlfriend became pregnant. He shouldn't have missed it.
He grew up in a church environment and his girlfriend's
father was a pastor. He shouldn't have missed grace, but
somehow it didn't get communicated. Carrying around
the guilt and shame of a secret for decades takes a toll
on a man's heart.

When the secret about my uncle Dave's son came
out, it was overwhelming for him. For decades he had
lived with the weight of it and the fear of people finding
out. What would my dad, his older brother, say? How
would his parents, my grandparents, respond? Would

they feel cheated out of knowing their grandchild? And what about his daughter, my cousin? She had grown up as an only child. She had always wanted a brother. But he never told her. He never told anyone.

And what about Wes? My uncle Dave had to think that his son would be angry at him. He could have felt abandoned and rejected his entire life. But now there was no hiding.

Sometimes our sin stays hidden because we are in denial or because our pride has blinded us to it. But oftentimes we try to keep our sin a secret because we just can't deal with what we've done. So we do our best not to think about the mistakes we've made or the sins we've committed, and we try to steer clear of God. How could he possibly forgive us when we can't even forgive ourselves?

Before Adam and Eve sinned in the Garden of Eden, the Bible says they lived life *naked and unashamed*. But the moment sin came on the scene, they were ashamed and did their best to hide from God.

Sometimes when our secret sin gets exposed and we can no longer hide it, then *we* go into hiding. As much as possible, we do our best to avoid the people who know. Shame becomes our constant companion who relentlessly whispers, *You're not worthy of forgiveness. You don't deserve a second chance.*

But here's a surprising characteristic about grace— *grace chases you*. You can run away and hide, but grace is relentless. Grace will chase you down. That's what's happening to some of you right now, and you don't even know it. With every word you read, grace is gaining ground.

> *You can run away and hide, but grace is relentless. Grace will chase you down.*

As a pastor, I love witnessing the moment grace finally catches up to someone's mess. The phrase I use to describe that moment is "beautiful collision." Those two words don't seem to go together. *Collision* brings to mind words like *broken*, *busted*, and *wrecked*—not typically words that fit with beautiful. But the Gospels are full of beautiful collisions. When a broken, busted, and wrecked life collides with Jesus, it's a beautiful thing.

## Crash Course with Grace

In John 4 we find ourselves at an intersection where a beautiful collision will soon take place. Jesus is traveling on his way to another city. John tells us in John 4:4 that "he had to go through Samaria." That seems like a strange way to put it. At the time, Jews would go out of their way to not go through Samaria. They would typically go around it and try to steer clear of any Samaritans. There was a lot of prejudice and hatred between the Jews and the Samaritans. They tried hard to have nothing to do with each other, to the point that if a first-century Jewish person read this, he would think John was making the point that Jesus *had* to go through Samaria because he had no other choice. Maybe a road was closed or traffic was backed up from so many people going around Samaria that he *had* to go through it.

Imagine if you asked a husband, "What did you do on your date last night?" He's not going to simply say, "I went to Yankee Candle and smelled candles." That would be awkward for everyone. If he admits to it at all, he's more likely to say, "I had to go to Yankee Candle and smell the different candles." The phrase *had to go* is important. He's making it clear that he was going against his will. He didn't have an option. He was forced into it. That's how a Jewish reader of the time would have heard this, but as you and I read the story, it seems clear that Jesus wasn't *forced* to go to Samaria, as if Jesus could be forced into anything.

Instead it seems like Jesus went out of his way to go to Samaria. "Had to go" seems to be used more in the sense that he had an appointment he had to keep. Like he looked on the calendar that was established before the creation of the world and saw he was supposed to be at a specific place at a specific time to meet a specific person. There was going to be a beautiful collision and God had it circled on his calendar. Grace chased this woman down and caught up with her at a well outside of town.

Jesus *had to go* to Samaria. He arrives around noon, in the heat of the day. He comes to the well and sits down to rest while his disciples go into town and get some food. It's an unusual time and place to meet someone. People would come to the well in the morning hours or in the late evening, not at noon when the sun was beating down. But then he sees the person he is waiting on. A woman arrives at the well to get some water. It was an unusual time for such a chore, but it was also uncommon that she was alone. In those days women would go to the well together, in the same way that women today are rarely seen going into a restroom alone.

What we soon discover is that this woman has a rough past and a bad reputation. It's hard to say if the reason she's alone is because she avoided people or they avoided her. It was probably mutual. She had grown tired of the judgmental looks and the whispers behind her back. So she went by herself, with only her shame and rejection to keep her company.

When she arrives, Jesus asks her for a drink, and she's not sure how to respond. She's taken aback that he, a Jewish man, would speak to her, a Samaritan woman, and she calls him on it.

"You are a Jew and I am a Samaritan woman. How can you ask me for a drink?" . . . Jesus answered her, "If you knew the gift of God and who it is that asks you for a drink, you would have asked him and he would have given you living water." (vv. 9–10)

Now she's really confused. She's thinking in terms of physical water for her physical thirst, so she points out that Jesus doesn't even have a bucket to draw water with. And Jesus explains to her that he is the living water and that if she drinks this water she'll never thirst again.

She's still not exploring the metaphor. He's not making sense to her. So Jesus decides to be a little more direct with her.

> He told her, "Go, call your husband and come back."
>
> "I have no husband," she replied.
>
> Jesus said to her, "You are right when you say you have no husband. The fact is, you have had five husbands, and the man you now have is not your husband. What you have just said is quite true." (vv. 16–18)

Well, that's uncomfortable. I think at this point she might be ready to go back to talking in metaphors. Jesus doesn't step away from the truth. He describes the reality of what she's done and the mess that her life has become. The well of relationships that she keeps drawing from isn't quenching her thirst, and Jesus isn't going to politely pretend that everything is OK when he knows that everything is not OK. If she's going to receive his grace, she needs to stop hiding in her sin.

This is hard, and I know we want to find another way, but here's the truth: before we collide with the grace of God, we must collide with the truth of our own sin. I wonder what hard truth Jesus would say to you and to me. Maybe he would say:

Your short temper keeps everyone around you on edge, and bitterness toward you is growing in your family.

Your drinking has gotten out of control. It's affecting a lot more people than just you.

Your porn problem is killing any chance of intimacy you have in your marriage.

Your flirting is leading you down a path that will devastate your family.

You're allowing your heart to fall for a girl who's causing you to fall away from me.

You're choosing your live-in boyfriend over your relationship with me. It's going to have to be one or the other.

You're going deeper into debt to feel better about yourself, but the water out of that well isn't going to satisfy you.

Your self-righteous and legalistic spirit is causing the people at your job to stay away from me.

Your judgmental attitude and your harsh tone are costing you a relationship with your grandkids.

Jesus speaks some difficult truths. It's the part of the collision with grace that we do our best to avoid. And like any of us would do, the woman at the well tries to steer the conversation away from her sin and shame.

> "Sir," the woman said, "I can see that you are a prophet. Our ancestors worshiped on this mountain, but you Jews claim that the place where we must worship is in Jerusalem." (vv. 19–20)

## False Assumptions

Let's push *pause* on our story and talk about some false assumptions this woman made about Jesus. These are the same assumptions that can cause us to miss his grace in our own lives.

### *Assumption #1: Jesus wants nothing to do with me.*

If your assumption about Jesus is that he doesn't have any interest in you, then there's a good chance you've never had much interest in him. Said another way, it's not that you don't want grace. Who wouldn't want grace? It's that you're convinced grace doesn't want you.

Feeling rejected can be one of the worst feelings to experience. When someone experiences rejection early and often, they quickly learn to build up walls to keep people from getting close. Given this woman's history of husbands, she was likely careful to avoid putting herself in a position of vulnerability. After all, you don't run the risk of rejection if you never give someone a chance to hurt you.

But Jesus went out of his way to be with this woman. Grace chased her down because that's what grace does.

After preaching at one of our Saturday-night services, I was standing down front as we worshiped. A man came to talk to me. I could tell he had been crying and was still a little emotional. He told me his name, and I asked how I could pray for him.

He cried his way through his answer. "Well, my wife has left me. It's my fault. I've done some really stupid things. I haven't treated her the way she deserves. She tried to tell me, but I just wouldn't listen. Would you pray that God would forgive me and my wife would forgive me? I know I'm ready to make some changes, but I'm not sure that God would want me here after the mess I've made of things."

He was assuming that his mistakes were greater than God's grace and that Jesus wouldn't want anything to do with him. I prayed for him and asked God to intervene in his marriage. I prayed that God would draw him and his wife back together again. I asked God to fight for him and for his marriage. But more than anything, I prayed for his relationship with Jesus, that he would know it wasn't an accident he was in church and that God wasn't rejecting him but was ready to help him.

After I prayed I asked him if this was where he went to church. He explained, or rather confessed, that he hadn't been to church since he was a kid. I said, "Oh, does your wife go here?" He explained that she didn't go to church either. Then I asked him what made him come and he said, "I don't know. I was driving by and just felt like I *had to go*."

I think I understood what he meant. I connected him to a man who presented the gospel to him, prayed with him, and got some information from him so we could follow up.

On Sunday morning, the very next day, I had finished with my message and was standing down front as the service was wrapping up. Two ladies came down to talk with me. It turns out they were sisters. One sister was comforting the other, who was clearly going through something difficult.

Before I had a chance to ask for her name or why she had come down, she explained, "I haven't been to church in a long time. I hope it's OK that I'm here. Last night I was so upset and my sister said I had to come this morning."

She asked me to pray for her husband, because they had recently separated. She asked if I would pray that God would soften his heart, because she didn't think he cared anymore.

At this point my heart was pounding. I said to her, "I didn't get a chance to get your name. Can you tell me your name?"

Do you ever get the feeling that God kind of winks at you?

I excitedly told her that her husband had come forward in tears just the night before. He had repented and asked God for help. I could tell she was having a hard time believing it. It was a beautiful collision, and grace was flying everywhere.

Both of them were making the assumption that God had given up on them and it was too late. They presumed that their marriage was too much of a mess and that he wouldn't want to have anything to do with it. But God made it clear that he was ready to meet them right where they were.

### Assumption #2: Jesus is more interested in religion than me.

Did you notice what the woman at the well does in the conversation? She tries to distract Jesus by talking about religion. She tries to avoid this collision by engaging him in some religious argument that could be debated endlessly. These days grace often gets overlooked because the church gets caught up in religious arguments and interpretive differences.

I'm amazed at how easy it is for us to become distracted with religious or even pseudoreligious arguments. I think we are especially prone to this when what we are studying gets a little uncomfortable.

Like the woman at the well, we have a tendency to get religious when Jesus starts to get a little too personal. I run into this as a preacher so often that I've developed a bit of a theory about it. The more people obsess over issues that clearly fall under the umbrella of theological interpretation or opinion, the more likely it is they're trying to keep Jesus from getting too personal in some area of their lives.*

I used to get distracted by this quite a bit. Someone would email me and go off on some interpretative detail they felt like I missed, and I'd fire off an email and defend my interpretation, and we'd go back and forth. I don't do this much these days. I'm not saying I never do it. If you want to try it, you're welcome to, but I rarely come out to play anymore. I've learned that when someone is especially determined to talk about religion, it's often because they are desperately trying to keep Jesus from getting too personal.

The Samaritan woman falsely assumes Jesus will be more interested in religion than her, so she tries to draw Jesus into a religious debate.†

*The more you don't like this theory, the more you reinforce it. Just sayin'.

†Spoiler alert: Engaging the Son of God in a theological debate is not an effective strategy.

*Assumption #3: He's making an offer that's too good to be true.*

This woman doesn't believe in water that will forever quench her thirst. Again, consider her history. She has had all kinds of men make her all kinds of promises and she's skeptical. She's cynical. She doesn't trust a man who seems to be promising more than he could possibly deliver.

She makes a number of false assumptions about Jesus and the gift he offers her. Those assumptions keep her from getting too close. Each assumption is like a brick in the wall that separates her from grace. And as their conversation continues she's ready to be done, so she tries to wrap it up.

> The woman said, "I know that Messiah" (called Christ) "is coming. When he comes, he will explain everything to us." (v. 25)

Don't miss the irony. She says to Jesus, *I know that when Jesus comes he'll make things clear.* And I don't know for sure, but I'm fairly certain Jesus couldn't help but give a slight smile when he said to her,

> I, the one speaking to you—I am he. (v. 26)

This is the only time in his entire life when Jesus voluntarily and candidly tells someone he is the Messiah, the Son of God. And it's to this Samaritan woman with a bad reputation who's been married five times and is now living with some other guy. How's that for grace?

## Chased by Grace

When the truth about your life is hard to face, when you've made such a mess of things you don't even know where to start cleaning up, when you can't forgive yourself, and guilt and shame are your constant companions, it's hard to imagine that grace is for you. Believe me, I get it.

Some of you think that the worst thing that could happen to you is that your sins will be found out and your secrets will be exposed. You're afraid that someone's going to bring up something you did a long time ago. You don't want anyone to know, and since God already knows, you do your best to avoid him. You think the worst thing that could happen is that you get found out and are forced to confront the truth.

*The worst thing that could happen is that you spend your life trying to outrun God because you think he's chasing you to collect what you owe—when he's really chasing you to give you what you could never afford.*

But that's not the worst thing. The worst thing that could happen is that you go through your life and *nobody knows*. No one ever finds out. You just carry the weight of your guilt and shame around with you everywhere. The worst thing that could happen is that you spend your life trying to outrun God because you think he's chasing you to collect what you owe—when he's really chasing you to give you what you could never afford.

## Father and Son

My uncle Dave and his son Wes began to talk from time to time, and after a few months they decided it was time to meet. My uncle lived in Missouri and Wes lived in Virginia, so they planned to meet at my house in Kentucky. We turned it into a miniature family reunion, and my grandparents and other extended family members were all there, excited to meet Wes.

I'll never forget standing in my driveway and watching as Wes pulled up with his beautiful family and my nervous uncle started walking toward their minivan. Wes stepped out, and we all wiped away the tears as we watched a father and son embrace for the first time.

I was too far away to hear what words were exchanged, but Wes gave my uncle a gift. A little later someone told me it was a watch. My uncle was really moved by the gift, but I didn't quite understand why it meant so much to him. Don't get me wrong; the watch seemed like a thoughtful gift, but I just didn't understand why it would cause such an emotional response.

Later that day my dad brought the watch over and showed it to me. It was a nice watch, as far as watches go, but I still didn't understand. Then my dad told me to turn it over. On the back there were two words engraved. Two words that have the power to change everything.

Pure Grace

## Pure Grace

The grace effect soon began to change my uncle. The weight of his shame and guilt suddenly fell from him. His hard heart became softer. Not long after this he ended a conversation we had by saying he loved me. He had never told me that before. He has become active in a church, and the pastor has become one of his good friends.

Maybe what surprises me most is that I get to tell you this story. I didn't think my uncle would be comfortable with me sharing this story with you. After all, when he worked so hard for so long to keep it a secret, I was sure he wouldn't want me to share it with the world. But I was wrong. That was exactly what he wanted. When I emailed him and asked for his blessing to share the story, here was his response:

> Please feel free to share my situation in any way that will express God's love, mercy, and amazing grace to anyone who needs it.

When I read his response, it reminded me of the change that took place in the heart of the woman at the well. Before she met Jesus, she didn't want anyone to see her. She didn't want anyone to know, and if they knew, she didn't want to know that they knew. She could never forgive herself for what she had done or the person she had become. But then her life collided with grace, and suddenly she saw things differently.

> The woman left her water jar beside the well and ran back to the village, telling everyone, "Come and see a man who told me everything I ever did! Could he possibly be the Messiah?" So the people came streaming from the village to see him. (vv. 28–30 NLT)

When God's grace and mercy collide with our shame and guilt, it's messy but it's beautiful. Jesus knows everything you ever did, but he wants to make sure you know that his grace is greater.

# More Redemptive
# Than Your Regrets

It was a Thursday night and I was lying in bed next to my wife. She had already fallen asleep but I was awake, staring at the ceiling and thinking about my sermon for the weekend. The focus of my message was on learning to live with regrets. The grip of regret can be more than demoralizing; it can be paralyzing. We can't seem to move forward because we obsess over something that has already happened, something that can't be unwound or undone. A regret tends to focus on a specific moment, a time and place where you did or didn't do something, and now you have to live with the consequences.

As I lay there thinking and praying about my sermon, I suddenly heard a crash come from our bathroom. I hopped out of bed and ran in and saw that the full-length mirror that had been hanging on our closet door had fallen off and was in pieces on the floor. When that mirror fell, it exposed something I did that I deeply regretted.

It exposed a hole in the closet door.

How did the closet door end up with a hole in it? I was afraid you'd ask that, though I suspect you could probably guess. I got into an argument with my wife. To be honest, I don't even remember what it was about.* But I got angry, lost my temper, and punched a hole in the closet door.

I really didn't want to tell you that.

The whole thing happened in a matter of seconds, but it happened.

I wish it hadn't happened.

I wish I could go back and be a patient and gentle husband.

I wish I would have responded with humility and self-control.

But I didn't.

After it happened I hoped my wife would forget about it and that my kids wouldn't find out. I was afraid of what the people who listen to me preach or read my books

---

*She probably does. But I wasn't going to bring it back up.

would think of me, if they discovered what I had done. So the way I dealt with my regret was to cover up what I had done and try to forget about it. And so I went to the store and bought a long mirror and hung it on the door and pretended it never happened.

I don't know what caused the mirror to come off the door and crash into pieces. It had been there for over a year. I suppose the adhesive that was holding the mirror to the door wasn't strong enough and eventually couldn't hold it. That's a possibility, but I suspect God was listening to me pray about a sermon that would challenge people to deal with their regrets and decided to flick the mirror off the door to remind me I had some regrets of my own that needed to be brought out of the darkness and into the light of his healing grace.

I stood in the closet and looked at the hole in the door and then down at the broken mirror on the floor. I could see my own reflection in the broken pieces. The metaphor was hard for me to miss. I like to think of myself as a patient, kind, and humble man who doesn't take himself too seriously. That's how I see myself, and that's the image I want others to have of me—especially my wife. I bent down and started picking up the broken pieces of mirror. I couldn't help but see myself in the pieces—I wish I could go back and do it differently, but I'll forever be a husband who got mad and put his fist through a door.

The crash woke up my wife. She came into the closet and found me on my knees picking up the glass. I'm not much of a crier, but I was crying and she knew it wasn't because I was especially attached to that mirror. I'm not sure I had ever really told her I was sorry. But I was ready to repent. Through tears I told both her and God I was so sorry for what I had done. She walked over to me, and I rested my head on her stomach and cried. I felt her fingers running through my hair. Sharing my regret and repenting for what I had done, rather than covering it up or keeping it to myself, put me in a position to receive some grace, and we finished picking up the broken pieces together.

## Regret vs. Shame

When we miss grace and live with guilt, that guilt usually surfaces in regret and shame. Regret and shame can, and often do, go together. They are not mutually exclusive. But there is a difference between regret and shame. Simply put, regret is feeling bad about *something you have or haven't done*, while shame is feeling bad about *who you are or how you think you're perceived* by God and others.

So in the previous chapter we spent some time getting to know the woman at the well in John 4. I'm sure she had regrets, but her real struggle was living in the shadow of her shame. It wasn't that she was trying to overcome a mistake or a poor decision; it was that her life was being defined by those things. Shame is more connected to your identity, while regret tends to be about something specific you did or did not do.

Several times a year I'll visit a prison and lead a Bible study for the inmates. I'll often stay for a while after the study to visit and pray with these men. I've learned that many of them are carrying the heavy weight of regret. It keeps them up at night. They may know that God has forgiven them, but they are constantly reliving a specific moment when they did something they never thought they would do and are consumed by what it has cost them and the people they love. As one inmate told me, "I know I have been forgiven, but I can't stop thinking about how different my life would be if only I could go back and make a different choice."

That's regret.

My guess is most of us can think of an hour or two—or maybe a decade or two—of our lives that we would give just about anything to have back. We would do things differently. In hindsight we can see the effect of that sin in our lives and in the lives of people we love. Enough of the bill has come due that we realize the cost is much more than we ever thought possible. And we never thought about the price others would have to pay.

I've noticed that when people talk to me about their regrets they typically begin the sentence with these words: *If only I . . .*

I recently came across a website called "Secret Regrets" that lists tens of thousands of posts from people expressing regret for something they did. Here are a few examples:

- "I regret when you were a baby and I was eighteen that my boyfriend was violent and I was too scared to stand up for you and me and they took you away. That was twenty years ago and I think about you every day."
- "I regret complaining about us walking too slowly and you leaning on me for balance. It was so much harder for you being handicapped. I was just a kid, and I'm sorry, Mom."
- "I regret that I never told you kids 'I love you' when you were growing up. I regret that for some reason I still can't say those words."
- "I regret that I was a self-centered mother who didn't let you help me in the kitchen because I didn't want it to get messy."

And the list goes on. Some are less specific:

- "I regret giving you my heart when all you wanted was my body."
- "I regret that I never saved any money and I'll never be able to retire."

- "I regret that I never told you how I felt."
- "I regret that I didn't fight for us."
- "I regret how much time I spent complaining and criticizing."

If there is one thing we have in common, it's that all of us have some regrets. We all wish we could go back and do some things differently.

Around three years ago I was about twenty thousand words into a book and somehow the document got corrupted. Every letter of every word on every page had been replaced by one of these: *. When I see these *, whatever these * are, I feel nauseated. I was fairly sure my publisher wasn't going to accept the book if the first four chapters were all **********. That document represented hundreds of hours of work. I was in a panic to get it back. I knew that it had been backed up recently, and I was hopeful I'd be able to recover most of my work. I got an IT guy on the phone. He told me not to worry and walked me through how to use a program on my Macbook called "Time Machine." Somehow, I assume through the combination of dark magic and a flux capacitor, I was able to go back in time on my computer to before the document was corrupted. It was like it never happened.

Wouldn't it be helpful if God equipped every human with a "Time Machine" function? How would you use it? Maybe you would go back to before you ever spoke those words to a sibling. Maybe you would go back to before you had the affair. Maybe you would go back to right before you took that first drink. Or right before you walked out on your family. Or right before you accepted your ex-boyfriend's Facebook request. Or right before you agreed to go on that first date. Or right before you walked into the abortion clinic.

You may not be locked up behind bars, but that doesn't mean you're not a prisoner. Most of us are desperate to be free from the guilt and regrets that imprison us.

## Regret, Remorse, and Repentance

The Bible tells us of a night when two of the disciples did something they never thought they would do. It was the night of Jesus's arrest. Jesus had been with his disciples in the upper room. Judas left the meal to betray him. He met with Jewish officials to make final arrangements for Jesus to be handed over to them.

But Judas isn't the only disciple who will betray Jesus on this night. Jesus warned the other disciples, "This very night you will all fall away on account of me" (Matt. 26:31). When Peter heard this, he was indignant. He passionately objected, but Jesus told him, "Truly I tell you, this very night, before the rooster crows, you will disown me three times" (v. 34). And then Peter doubled down on his commitment: "Even if I have to die with you, I will never disown you" (v. 35).

The sun has gone down as Jesus leads his disciples through the streets of Jerusalem. They head out of the city through the eastern temple gate and toward the Mount of Olives. They reach an enclosed wooded area called Gethsemane. Jesus instructs his disciples to pray and then goes off by himself. He knows the horror that awaits him, and in the quietness of the night he cries out to his Dad.

Jesus must have come to the Garden of Gethsemane to pray somewhat often, because Judas knows right where to find him. He leads a group of some six hundred men into the garden to arrest Jesus. Judas has arranged a signal so that all of them would know which one was Jesus. And so he walks up to Jesus and betrays him with a kiss. The soldiers move in to arrest Jesus. The disciples are outnumbered sixty to one; they don't have a chance. But Peter grabs a butcher's knife, likely the one that had been used earlier in the evening to carve the Passover lamb, and takes a swing at the servant of the high priest. Peter tries to take off his head but manages to lop off only an ear. I'm guessing Peter had a few holes in his closet door. Jesus immediately steps in and puts a stop to what Peter is doing. He picks the ear up, disconfects it, and reattaches it to the servant.

Once Jesus is under arrest, all but two of the disciples flee. Peter and John follow Jesus from a safe distance.

At some point the two separate, and Peter waits in the courtyard of the high priest to see what will happen to Jesus. That's when a slave girl recognizes Peter and asks if he is one of the disciples. And Peter does what he promised he would never do—he denies Jesus. Then he makes his way over to a fire where he stands with a number of others trying to stay warm. Again he is recognized and again he denies even knowing Jesus.

A little later Peter is recognized a third time, and for a third time Peter denies knowing Jesus. In fact, he even swears on the penalty of hell that he doesn't know Jesus. But his swearing is interrupted by the crowing of a rooster. At that very moment Jesus is being led through the courtyard. He has been badly beaten. His face is bloodied and swollen. Luke 22:61 tells us:

> At that moment the Lord turned and looked at Peter. Suddenly, the Lord's words flashed through Peter's mind: "Before the rooster crows tomorrow morning, you will deny three times that you even know me." (NLT)

Peter comes to his senses. He realizes what he has done. The very thing he swore he would never do, he did.

> Peter left the courtyard, weeping bitterly. (v. 62 NLT)

As Jesus continues through a series of illegal and unjust trials, we're told that Judas is also filled with remorse.

He's overwhelmed with regret and is desperate to make things right. He goes to the chief priests and elders and throws the money into the temple. "I have sinned," he confesses to them, "for I have betrayed innocent blood" (Matt. 27:4).

Both Peter and Judas are filled with guilt and regret over what they have done. If they could go back in time and undo their mistakes they would, but they can't. You can't. You did the one thing you promised yourself you would never do, and it can't be undone. Maybe you didn't do it once. Maybe you did it three times. Maybe you've lost track of how many times.

*Unfortunately, when we come face-to-face with our guilt, we often do everything we can to avoid remorse.*

Now it feels like a few days, or a few hours, or a few minutes, or maybe just a few seconds will define the rest of your life.

*Our regrets should lead to remorse.* That's the right response when we are confronted with our sin. God's grace won't leave you there, but that's where God's grace will most often find you. Unfortunately, when we come face-to-face with our guilt, we often do everything we can to avoid remorse.

Here are some of the common ways I see people deal with their regrets:

1. *Rationalization.* Some of the common rationaliza-
   tions that I hear: "I'm not hurting anyone/I can't
   help the way I feel/God made me this way/God
   wants me to be happy." You can always tell when
   someone is rationalizing because you get the feeling that they are trying to convince themselves that
   something is OK when they know it's not.

2. *Justification.* This usually takes the form of blaming anything or anyone but oneself. Many people
   deal with regret by explaining all the ways it's not
   their fault so it's not their responsibility. "If my
   parents weren't so permissive/If my parents weren't
   so strict/If my wife wasn't so critical/If my husband
   wasn't so inattentive/If my boss wasn't so unfair/If
   the culture wasn't so corrupt."

3. *Comparisons.* We touched on this in chapter 1, but
   people try to make themselves feel better about
   their regrets by comparing themselves to others. I
   think this is one of the reasons people love gossip
   magazines and reality TV. Nothing makes us feel
   like what we've done isn't that big of a deal like
   hearing about what other people have done. It
   somehow eases our regret when we can say, "Well
   at least I didn't _____."

4. *Distraction.* This is a big one. We never stop long
   enough to look at ourselves in the mirror. We never

take the time to reflect upon the decisions we've made. We fill up every inch of our lives with work, relationships, and entertainment. If we ever happen to have a few spare seconds, we instinctively whip out our cell phones and play games or surf the web.

5. *Escapism.* This is a hard-core form of distraction. A person can't deal with the regret they feel so they pop a few pills, smoke some weed, get drunk, or pull out the credit card and go on a shopping spree. We self-medicate trying to treat our guilt and numb the pain of what we have done, if only for a while.

Both Peter and Judas own their mistakes. They admit where they went wrong. They allow their regrets to lead them to remorse. But they deal with their remorse differently. Judas returns the thirty pieces of silver he had taken for betraying Jesus. It's good that he tried to make things right. As much as possible, we should take responsibility for what we've done. The problem is that there is very little we can do about many of the regrets we have. That tends to be one of the most significant reasons we have such a hard time living without regrets. Judas realizes he can't undo what has been done. He can't fix things or put the pieces back together, and the Bible tells us that he went out and hanged himself (Matt. 27:5).

Judas couldn't deal with his regrets. He was convinced that his regrets were greater than God's redeeming grace. He couldn't live with the weight of what he had done, so he killed himself. Most people won't deal with their regrets by way of suicide, but I'm convinced that many people are slowly killing themselves with regret.

Peter, like Judas, is filled with regret, but Peter repents. Regret should lead to remorse, and *remorse should lead to repentance*. I don't want to read too much into this, but in my mind it's significant that both Peter and Judas are filled with remorse, but we read that only Peter wept. The Message paraphrases Luke 22:62 as, "He went out and cried and cried and cried." Maybe the reason this catches my attention is because I have learned to look for tears as a sign of repentance. It's one of the questions I ask men who come and confess a sin: "Have you cried about it?" Maybe it seems like an odd question, but in my experience tears can have incredible healing power when it comes to dealing with our regrets. John Chrysostom put it this way: "The fire of sin is intense, but it is put out by a small amount of tears, for the tear puts out a furnace of faults and cleans our wounds of sins."

Second Corinthians 7:10 makes a possible distinction between the way Judas and Peter dealt with their

> I'm convinced that many people are slowly killing themselves with regret.

regrets: "Godly sorrow brings repentance that leads to salvation and *leaves no regret*, but worldly sorrow brings death" (emphasis added).

One early morning, after Jesus had risen from the dead, Peter was out with some of the other disciples fishing. This is what he did for a living before he became a full-time follower of Jesus. Maybe he had returned to the business feeling like a failure after denying the one he had left everything to follow. Maybe he had repented of his sin and been forgiven but would be forced to live the rest of his life with his regrets—thinking of what could have been and how God might have used him, if only . . .

From the boat Peter saw a lone figure walking on the shore about a hundred yards away. The man called out to the boat, "Have you caught anything?" Peter and the others responded, "No, nothing." The man on the shore said, "Throw your nets on the other side." The fishermen complied and their nets were full of fish (see John 21:4–6).

Peter realized it was Jesus, and he couldn't wait for the boat to get back to shore. He dove into the water and swam to him. Jesus was cooking breakfast, and they gathered around a charcoal fire. Have you ever noticed how a distinctive smell can bring back a memory? The stench of a locker room reminds you of football, the peculiar odor of a factory reminds you of a summer job, a distinctive perfume can remind you of your first date with your wife. I wonder if the smell of those coals triggered in Peter's mind the last time he had stood around a fire—when he had denied Jesus.

As they stood around that fire, three times Jesus asked Peter, "Do you love me?" Three times Peter affirmed his love. Then Jesus said, "Feed my sheep" (see vv. 15–17). Jesus is telling Peter that he doesn't have to be imprisoned by his regrets. Jesus still has a great plan for Peter. Grace has the power to redeem regret.

## A Trophy of God's Grace

The morning after we picked up the broken pieces of the mirror that had fallen off the closet, I told my wife that I was feeling like God wanted me to share with the church the story of me punching a hole in the door and then covering it up. I asked her if she was OK with that. I realized that the story would be embarrassing for her. She might not want thousands of people to know that she's married to a guy who punched a hole in her closet door. I was secretly hoping she would say no, because I was sure God would understand and let me off the hook.

But when I asked for her permission, she said, "If you think that's what God wants you to do, then you should."

I told her the truth. "I'm just a little afraid of what people might think of me." With a little laugh, she replied, "Trust me, we're not the only ones with a hole in our door."

That weekend I stood up to talk about the difference between living with regrets and repenting so that we can be set free by grace. I came clean and told the church that their preacher had lost his temper and punched a hole in the door. When the service was over, I saw one of our church leaders walking over to me. I looked down as he approached. I was embarrassed and not sure what he was going to say. He gave me a hug and said, "No one knows this, but there's a hole behind a picture in my bedroom." We talked for a few minutes, and by the time we were finished I looked up to see five more guys waiting to talk to me. You'll never guess what they wanted to tell me. When my wife said we weren't the only ones with a hole in our door, I assumed she meant that metaphorically, but after every service that weekend I had men lining up to tell me about a literal hole.

If you come to my house today and walk into my closet, you will still find a hole in the door. I never replaced the door. I didn't cover it back up with another mirror. I decided to leave it exposed because a strange thing happened. That hole in the door, which I wanted to hide because it reminded me of something I regretted, started to remind me of how much I am loved. A busted closet door became a trophy of God's grace.

Grace is greater than a hole in my closet door.

# Your Grace Effect

As you come to the end of this little book, you've learned some things about me. Some are things I'm not especially proud of, but I'm glad to tell you about them because I'm more excited about the grace I have experienced than I am embarrassed by the sins I have committed. The most important thing about me isn't what I have done but rather what God has done for me through Jesus.

I find myself wondering about you. I'm wondering if you're carrying around some guilt that has weighed you down for too long. I wonder if you're dealing with some brokenness you'd like God to heal.

I also find myself wondering how it is that you ended up reading this little book. This may sound a little superstitious to you, but I don't believe it's an accident you're reading this. Maybe you could give me a rational explanation: a friend or family member passed it along, a stranger whose name you've already forgotten gave it to you, a church you were visiting was handing them out, maybe the inmate who was in your cell before you left it behind, or maybe it was left in the pocket of the seat in front of you on the airplane. I've heard all those stories before, and plenty more like them. In fact, I've heard them enough that it would be hard to convince me it's a coincidence that you are reading this now. I believe you were meant to read this.

That wouldn't surprise me. Not at all. We've already discussed just how far God has gone so that you could experience his grace in your life. If he didn't even spare his only son, then wouldn't it also make sense that he might work it out so you would be reading these words right now?

He wants you to experience your own grace effect. He wants to forgive you for the things you've done and make something beautiful out of your brokenness.

You're not too guilty.

You're not too broken.

It's not too late.

You've already read this far, but can I ask you to go one step further?

This will take a little more courage than reading words on a page. I'd like to ask you to call and talk to someone about what it means to put your faith in Jesus.

You can call this number right now: 1-888-633-3446.

You'll be calling a reputable ministry called Need Him Global (needhim.org). The folks there are ready to talk to you, pray with you, and help you experience God's grace in your life.

# Notes

**Chapter 1  More Forgiving Than Your Guilt**

1. Jeremy W. Peters, "Bloomberg Plans a $50 Million Challenge to the N.R.A.," *New York Times*, April 15, 2014, http://www.nytimes.com/2014/04/16/us/bloomberg-plans-a-50-million-challenge-to-the-nra.html.

2. Saint Augustine, *Confessions*, vol. 5 (UK: Penguin, 2003), 103.

**Kyle Idleman** is teaching pastor at Southeast Christian Church in Louisville, Kentucky, the fifth largest church in America, where he speaks to more than twenty thousand people each weekend. He is the bestselling and award-winning author of *Not a Fan* as well as *Gods at War* and *The End of Me*. He is a frequent speaker for national conventions and in influential churches across the country. Kyle and his wife, DesiRae, have four children and live on a farm in Kentucky, where he doesn't do any actual farming.

# CONNECT
# WITH **KYLE**!

---

📘 KyleIdleman

🐦 @KyleIdleman

**KyleIdleman.com**

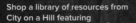